# *Metal Embossing:*
## *Templates and Ideas*

Hand-Tooled Pewter Repousse

Halos for Saints and Iconography

## *Mary Jane Miller*
## *and ValentinGomez*

Historically, the many well-known icons of the Virgin Mary included hand tooled pewter and silver halos. For iconographers today, painting saints with halos embellished in pewter is still a thriving art form in many countries, especially in Mexico. Inspired Byzantine iconographers use metal foil for embossing pewter, chasing and engraving to accent sacred art. Valentin Gomez and Mary Jane Miller's new book Embossing Metal: Templates and Beginner Techniques for tooling metal foil pewter is an essential resource. Russian and Greek iconography employ countless elaborate design styles.

We offer the book as guidance, it is a collection of icon templates for those devoted to traditional fine craftsmanship. Beautifully embellished halos have been a Byzantine iconographical legacy and tradition for centuries.

Mary Jane Miller is a first class teacher and Iconographer with decades of experience. Her collection includes more than 1,000 icons in the ancient practice of egg tempera. She speaks and consults on Byzantine style iconography in formal class settings, five day intensive silent icon painting retreats or one-on-one instruction and coaching.

She has been painting/writing icons and teaching since 1995. Her collections include the *Life of Christ* series, *The Mary Collection*, *In Light of Women Series, the Stations of the Cross* and *On Holy Ground*. Some people have identified her as a mystic without a monastery, others refer to her as rebellious. Her work is always theologically provocative. Mary Jane lives in San Miguel Allende, Mexico.

*Metal Embossing: Templates and Ideas*
All Text, Templates and Paintings by Mary Jane Miller
Hand tooled pewter repousse work by Valentin Gomez
Layout, and photography by Mary Jane Miller
www.millericons.com

# CONTENTS

## Introduction

# INTRODUCTION

Metal Embossing is known in Spanish as repujado. In French, they say repousse, they both mean to push. Metal embossing to make a riza or oklad, is an art form that has been around for centuries. Riza or oklad is a term used to describe the beautiful metal covers originally applied to icons so they could be protected and transported. Embossing metal imparts luster, radiance, to an otherwise flat appearance, adding intriguing dimension, texture, and value. The artful practice of repousse and egg tempera has quietly endured for centuries. Lavish embellishments of silver, gold, and jewels to accent the beauty of icons was a common practice in Russia around the 18th century.

This book is geared towards those of you in the iconography community interested in creating your own silver halos. The first section of the book discusses tools, supplies and technique. Tools and metal foil sheets are all you need to create beautiful designs. Each tool has its own character and purpose to help you press from the back to the front and flatten raised areas that get distorted. As you learn to refine the edges of your patterns, you will add a few more tools to accommodate increased skill. This book gives you a place to begin and inspires you to go further with practice.

After describing the tools and supplies, I give you basic techniques, step-by-step, to teach yourself how to create borders and halos to embellish your icons. The process is simple, and only requires investing hours of focused practice. After about ten hours of practice, you will begin to sense and feel the amount of pressure required to make fluid designs and texture. Experimenting will bring the best results and in no time you will be skilled enough to create beautiful work for embellishing your icons.

The second section of the book includes an assortment of templates. These templates can be photographed, copied, enlarged, or reduced. Expand the background or cut away a little to fit the size of your saint's image.

The last section is an assortment of finished icons by my husband, Valentin Gomez and myself. We are both self-taught iconographers and have been quietly working together for 26 years. His master craftsmanship fits perfectly to my hand-painted original Byzantine style icons. The collection is not exactly Byzantine Orthodox but follows much of the style and commitment. Examining the finished icons and the template will make clear to you how we arrive at a finished product. "Our dream is keep this style alive and add a few new icons to those existing in the world. We hope that this great sacred art tradition will continue in liturgy and prayer for a long time to come".

# MATERIALS FOR THE BEGINNER ARE NOT EXPENSIVE

In order to begin, you will need a few sheets of embossing foil, a set of tools, a sheet of glass, one thick piece of soft leather, and finishing liquids to clean and polish the completed product. The resource guide at the back of this book provides several suppliers to contact for materials. The same supplier will have a variety of embossing tools: styluses, refiners, paper stumps and an assortment of detailing tools you will all find of value. My recommendation is to start small. This means, buy enough to get going. Experiment and see if your heart and mind are up to learning this technique. Though it is easy; it requires commitment as all things do that are meaningful. You will notice your fingers do get tired. With practice the muscles get strong and the pain goes away. Even if you only do a few small halos you gain an appreciation for the dedicated work done by ancient masters.

Our book begins with simple instructions and illustrations for each tool. We master any craft or skill through practice and patience. You will refine your style and application with time. Additional suggestions, tips, sample patterns, templates, and examples of finished icons from our collection will assist you, providing inspiration and guidance.

## METAL FOIL MATERIALS LIST:

Parchment or tracing paper
Pencil and eraser a few sheets of pewter or metal foil
12" square sheet of glass
12" square sheet of soft leather or  piece of dense spongy mat
A selection of tools
Soap and water
Polish either, Knox silver Polish or Silva
polishing cloth
Filler for the back
Scissors
Exacto knife
Strong fingers
Time and ideas

# YOUR WORK SURFACE

You will work on the back and front of the metal sheet. For tooling you will need to work on two surfaces. Both surfaces must be larger than the pattern you draw on the metal. The hard surface could be an 18" hard plastic or glass square or smaller. The soft chamois leather could be 18" square or smaller. The black you see in the photo is black leather, you can also use any dense spongy surface. Rubber is too hard, regular sponge is too soft. Try several surfaces or look through the resource links to find a supplier. You will use the soft surface for the embossing and the hard surface to press the metal down flat. VIDEO in resource guide

Templates and Beginner Techniques

# THE BEST KIND OF METAL FOIL FOR EMBOSSING

The best results come from using pewter sheets. Many consider the cheaper tin foil sheets. In reality, that is a waste of time. It is easy to poke holes through thin metal by applying too much pressure and pressing too deep too fast. There is one video in the resource section that uses a tin can. VIDEO in resource guide It may be interesting to try that technique! You will find it is tough to achieve smooth curves and straight lines using a tin can, it is an inflexible metal. Use pewter sheets rather than less expensive metal sheets of aluminum, copper or tin. In the long run, you will gain more control and build up your skill.

When you move to the pewter you will be so happy, the finished product is superior quality. Coated pewter sheets are the best kind of metal for embossing because of its softness and manageability. The quality allows the tools to slide easily, achieving extraordinary dimension, volume, and visual beauty. When you buff and polish at the end, it will really shine. Begin by experimenting with small designs to get used to the material.

Aluminum, copper, or pewter embossing foils are sold by the sheet or roll depending on the supply house.Most companies will sell you a few feet if that is all you need to begin. I recommend 36 or 38 gauge metal. If you are a beginner, purchase slight amounts until you find the gauge and type that best suits you. A roll can be 12" x 25 ft. This is perfect for producing a collection.

## TOOL DESCRIPTIONS

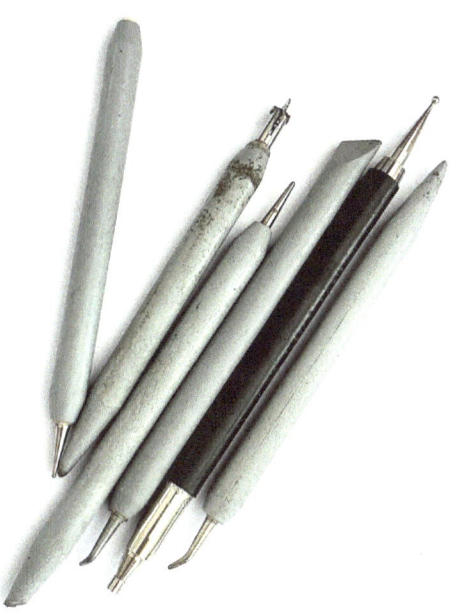

Tools for embossing are interesting. With repeated usage they become chosen friends. Valentin has many tools but only uses about 7 of them. Each one does something but no one does everything.

Six tools in this group make a fine set. Two chisels, one stylus, a nice soft round. The black one pictured is a ball and cup. First, you press down the ball end, then turn the tool around to press the cup end for flattening and shaping. There is a wheel tool that makes little dots all in a row. This one is versatile for texturing.

These are called paper stumps, they are cheap and indispensable. Use them to flatten the front side of your design without scratching the metal. The small one gets into corners easily. They can be sharpened in a pencil sharpener or with a knife.

The wooden egg is used to push deep hollowed out volumes and forms. Use this tool after you have your entire design finished for a more voluminous halo. It bends large areas in one stroke without ruining the detail.

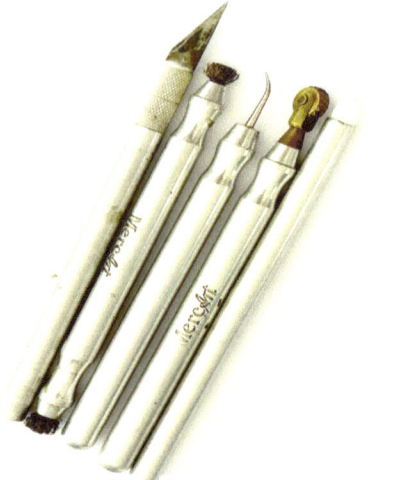

This assortment is more for finishing. Two steel brush tools for texture. One wheel tool that makes attractive edge patterns or cross section patterns in backgrounds.

One exacto knife for cutting the final design cleanly to fit the icon's image perfectly and snuggly. A stylus will also cut the metal. The white chisel tool is good for finishing and tightening up volumes.

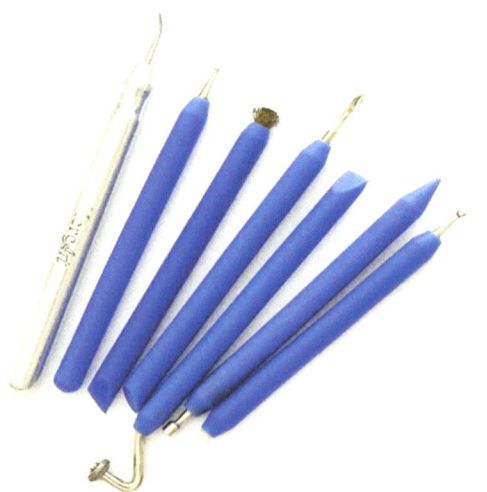

Small kits of tools are available and can be found in the resource links. This is a small package of 6 tools purchased for ten dollars in 2020. Contact me if you want me to send you a set for beginning your practice.

The stylus we added for quality and at an additional expense. A good stylus with a thin metal shape is ideal. We tried a dental tool that was fantastically thin and strong, but limited in capacity.

Templates and Beginner Techniques

# BEGINNING

Using regular scissors cut the metal foil 1/4 inch larger than the pattern of your design. Place the tracing paper with your pattern on the metal and tape it in place. Trace the pattern of your design onto the metal sheet using the hard acrylic or glass surface underneath. I like to use a ballpoint pen that no longer has ink in it for tracing. The round ball is perfect for getting a smooth line onto the metal through the transfer paper. When you remove the tracing paper, you see your design transferred onto the metal. After you have transferred your design, notice it leaves a small impression on the other side. The surface you have drawn on is, in fact, the back. I write "back" on the metal with a ' Sharpie ' so you remember. Remove the ink from the marker at the end with alcohol.

# WHEN YOU HAVE YOUR PATTERN DRAWN

Now, you change the hard surface you are working on, replacing it with the leather. With the drawing side up press into the metal with any tool. Normally you begin with your stylus tool to mark the designs of your drawing. The leather acts like a cushion allowing the pliable properties of the metal to expand. Push the metal to shape deep impressions. Working on a hard surface does not allow you to press to create a volume. To press down into the metal, you must work on the suede surface. Do not go too deep at first. Make your figures and forms gradually. Repeat the movements to refine and enlarge the form. You want to focus on one small section at a time. Turn over your metal sheet and change back to the hard acrylic plastic or glass beneath your piece. Flatten the areas you did not emboss using the paper stump tool.

*Explaining this is crazy, the best way to learn is to make small samples.*

To summarize, the process involves using certain tools to push out from the back while on the suade surface. Switch to the hard surface using other tools to flatten the distortions. Push out the metal to form raised areas and flatten the opposite side to clarify the design. The embossed areas rise out of the flat areas.

# DESIGN A SAMPLE FOR YOURSELF

Experiment with a design sample something simple. The first row uses the stylus and chisel tool, the second row is using several tools, and the third row uses only the stylus. The stylus will be the most useful and the hardest to dominate. Using a selection of tools will help you get acquainted with what each tool is capable of. As you experiment with the metal foil, you will grasp certain preferences and become proficient.

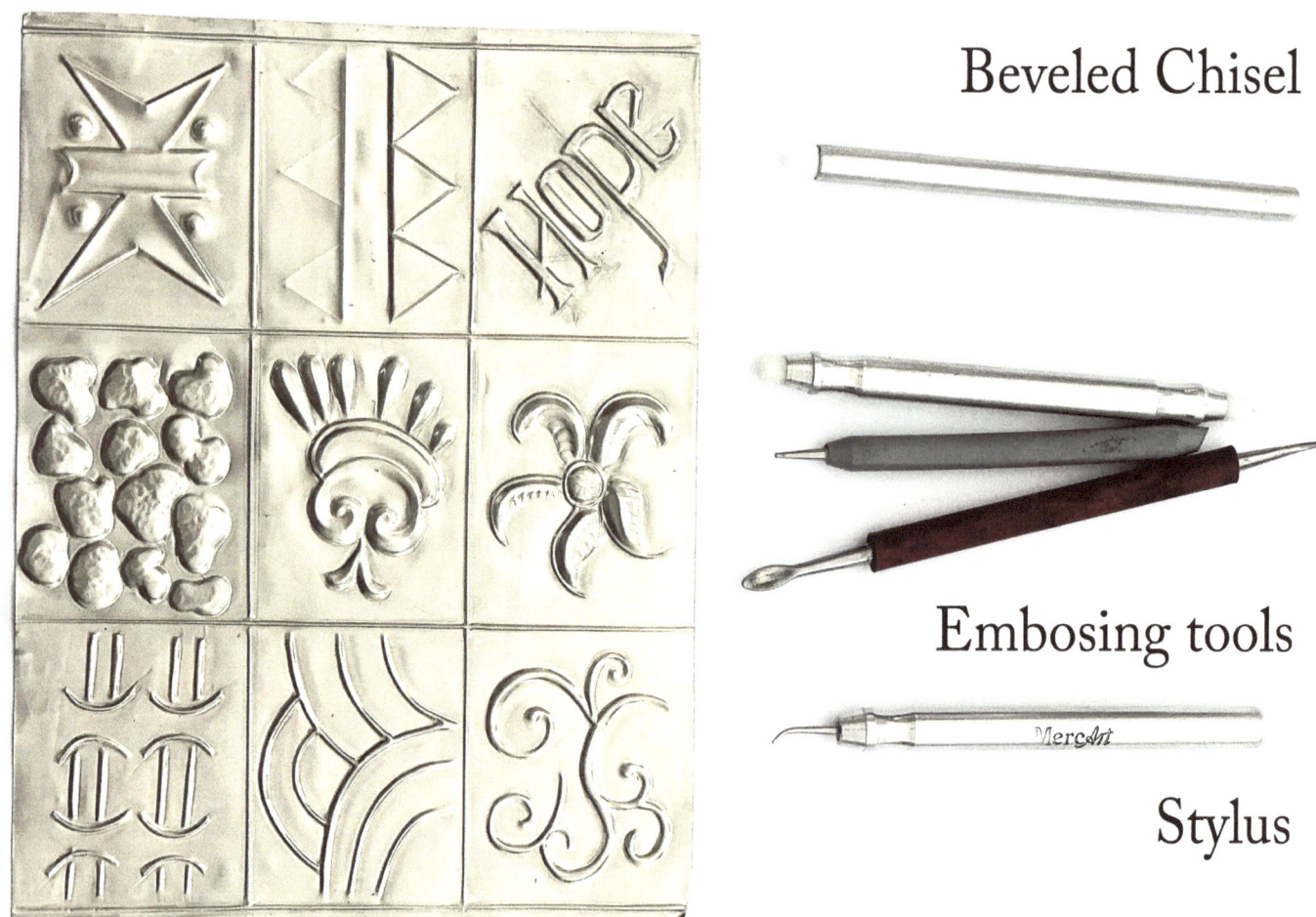

Beveled Chisel

Embosing tools

Stylus

# BEGIN EMBOSSING METAL

Push the metal to form your individual designs one small area at a time on top of the soft leather cushion. Turn it over onto the hard surface repeatedly to clean up the embossed lines. Smooth down any surface that is warped or distorted. Each side becomes distinct. In the beginning it can be confusing which side is which. Alternate working the back and the front refining each shape or embellishment to perfection. Make a sample of a few letters, this way you will really understand what is right side and wrong side.

Remember: pushing out the design is on leather, and cleaning/refining/flattening is on the glass or plastic surface. Use the paper stump, chisels or points to push the metal inside the embossed areas to smooth the shapes.
Use the stump on the hard plastic to run along the outside edges of each embossed shape. Clean up and refine all edges. Always be aware of the side you are working on. try to prevent scratching the metal on the good side. The reason for this is when you go to buff the metal it will not buff well if it is scratched.

# ADDING TEXTURE

When the detailing is finished and you have flattened the background with the paper stumps you are ready to add texture. Add texture or draw ++repetitive patterns on the flat surface. Scratch or etch with various tools. The scatched metal surface will retain more of the patina when work gets polished. This technique adds contrast to the overall design. Texture will pick up the dark patina and give a finished look to your design. Experiment by moving the brush tool back and forth or use the single point tool to move in a circular pattern. Compare this with parallel lines or cross-hatching. These movements enhance your design with more depth.

In the sample below note that the background surface on the left side are not fully flattened. Valentin did flatten the backgrounds before he applied the texture. Make sure you do not make this mistake, if so the background patters become irregular when applied to a bumpy surface.

# FINISHING

When you've finished all the lines, curlicues, and textures, your design is complete. Turn it over on the back side and fill the hollow areas using a filling compound applied with a spatula or pallet knife.

Each embossed area must be filled with paste to prevent the metal from getting dented. For years the car industry has used this technique to fill the dents in the car frame. Using a plastic spatula, spread the compound evenly so it is flat, like icing a cake. Let the paste dry for 30 minutes. The solidness of the paste will prevent your design from collapsing giving support to the once hollow areas

Easy to make recipe with a few house
hold ingredients.  Mix 1 cup of Talcum
Powder, 1/2 cup of Elmers glue, and 1/2 cup of acrylic paint. Add a few drops of water to get the correct consistency. Store in a Tupperware container.  Video link in the resource guide.
You Tube Title:  Making Your Own Texture Paste

# PATINA

Patina is similar to any antiquing process. In this case the metals are oxidized and when the highest areas are buffed the patina is left darker in the grooves and sunken areas.

First, wash the surface well with soap and water. When it is air dry, apply the liquid patina (muriatic acid) with a brush large enough to cover the surface quickly. The patina liquid changes the surface making it tarnish. It will turn your metal a dark gray, almost black. Move the brush into the corners. If it is slightly uneven at first usually in a few minutes it will get darker. If not, that is because the surface had grease from your hands, the metal needs to be cleaned well to avoid this. Wipe off the excess patina with a soft T shirt cloth. You can reapply the patina if you buff off too much.

Buff clean with Brasso or silver polish and the embossed areas should become bright with only a little effort.

Applying the patina takes practice to control the dark and light areas. Eventually, you will know what your preference and desired look is. I like the dark antique looking patinas and my husband likes the shiny bright silver finish. When the patina is dry, you are ready to buff. Polish your metal design with polishing paste like Knox or here in Mexico we use Silva, both are polish used for silver.

# CONSULTATIONS
# AND HELPFUL ASSISTANCE

For personal feedback, options, and constructive ideas or questions about applying embossed pewter to your icon we are available. The format can be as you choose. Send me a jpg image of the current work, and its actual dimensions and we will comment or design for you. We can send the parchment template that you fit onto the work. We can also create the actual repouse work and send it to you for you to attach to your icon. We can set up an hour ZOOM meeting, or SKYPE time to review your work and answer questions. We can share live conversational instruction and demonstrations if you can get to a workshop here in Mexico. I am available for helping you find your way to sharpen your intent. One-hour instruction can be scheduled through PayPal. Send me an email request and I'll send you the secure payment link. $30.00 US an hour.

It is always a fine idea to work out what part of your icon, candlestick, book cover or any project will receive embellishments. Many times I thought well Ill think about this later. Thinking is a form of planning the direction to go in.'It the silver is next to a light color it is less dramatic than beside a dark color. If you want to try cutouts in your metal the ground must be how you like it and not think you will paint it in r use gold leaf later.

# TEMPLATES

This section is for your use and exploration. Perhaps, cut the templates or switch border designs. Our riza or oklad designs are all original and one of a kind. Use any template as a pattern, adjusting it to your specific icon image. You have to plan carefully when selecting the template in order for the pewter to fit your image with accuracy. One important tip: Be careful to make sure the metal and the image fit to each other as anticipated. We have done several icons where the riza or oklad is the exact opposite of the icon. This happened because we began working on the wrong side, i.e. the saint's head bent to the left in the icon and to the right in the finished riza. This is even more important where lettering is concerned. Letter in relief can end up backwards.

In fact now that i think of it To get a clear understanding of back and front start with a sample of your initials. You will see clearly why the flipping from back to front is so important.

The halo samples are drawn on velum paper/ tracing paper. Originally using a pencil then you can refine with ink. The templets are offered as an idea of you to expand on, the halo will not fit any image of course, the idea is to begin somewhere, then expand the details, adding more lines on the outside or less to certain areas. This was a halo fit for Jesus. The one on the right for Mary and her Son.

Templates and Beginner Techniques

Templates and Beginner Techniques

Templates and Beginner Techniques

# BOARDERS AND BANDS FOR FRAMING

Designing boarders is a little like making paper dolls. Remeber as children we folded paper, cut a pattern or shape and then unfolded the paper. This will give you perfect segments all the same size.

Or, you can take one small very detailed design and repeat it. Section out divisions for how large a space you need to cover.

Designing boarders can be easy. Especially on the internet. Designing one strip by hand is tedious but the quality of line is more interesting. It does not look industrial like metal that has been stamped.

Rememeber the corners, they can become beautiful accents.
Small nuances, a stone or two and several variations even errors make it look hand made. Examining ancient iconography embellishments you can see what I mean.

NOTICE; this draft design is not complete. It lacks the circles around the outside and is not actually correctly centered. Works out your design in full on one side at the very least. That way you can fold the paper in half and trace the other side. When you get more experienced you will only have to refine one side and then flip it over to trace the other side. ALSO, remember lettering has to be in reverse. You will push it out from the back. I have goofed this up many times as it is part of the dyslexic experience.

Random ideas and simple template ideas. These round templates I used for the eye of God you see at the end of the book. These could also be inspiration for halo ideas. Keeping your designs simple at the beginning, that will help you develop style and skill. Bands at the top of an icon can be a beautiful accent
Corners can also be a stunning addition to any icon.
When you feel more advanced try covering the entire icon..

Templates and Beginner Techniques

Templates and Beginner Techniques

Templates and Beginner Techniques

Templates and Beginner Techniques

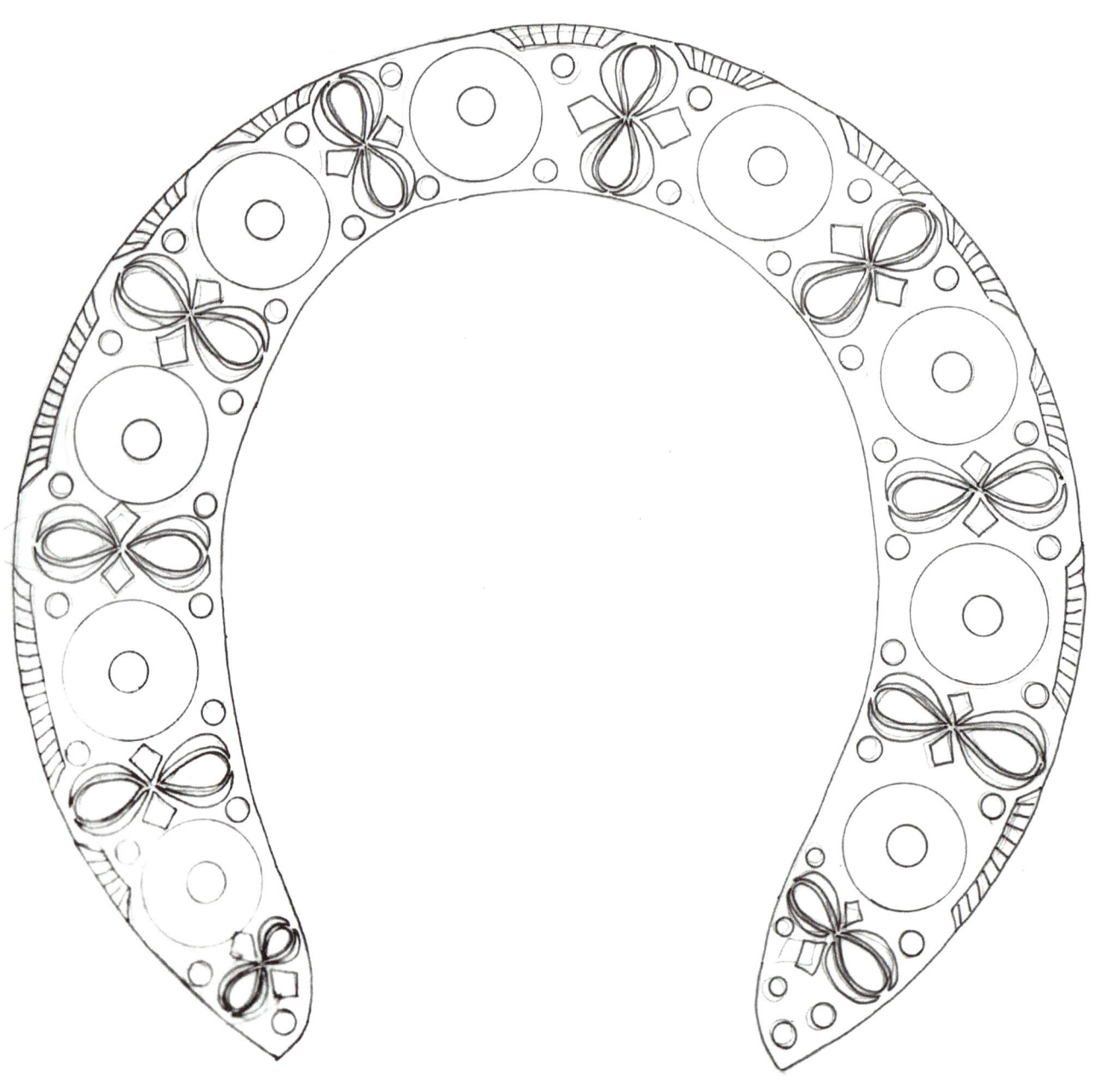

Templates and Beginner Techniques

# PLACING STONES

Placing stones can be done in two ways. After finishing the final design, washing, patina, and buffing of the estano you can cut holes in the appropriate place and embed the stone.

The stone or pearl will pop through the hole made in the metal and be exposed. Carve out a depression  and glue them into your gesso to keep them from moving. The  other way is to embed them in the estano. Place sticky-tape or glue on the back to keep them from falling out.

Either way, cut the wholes small and stretch the metal. This way you will have a natural looking bevel.

Templates and Beginner Techniques

Valentin Gomez

# ANCIENT EXAMPLES

It is an excellent idea to look at the ancient masters. Even if the work is not perfect they had some clever ideas and use of materials, They had less abundance than we have today, and therefore the desire for beads or pearls to match was of little consequence. the effect is lovely and the overall look is very handmade.

Notice the one on the bottom left. It would have employed a standard pre-pressed ' commercial laminate.The design is cut and placed without much care. Even so, the effect is marvelous. The virgin above is striking. The halo dominates the icon. It was paced afterward. I think so because the lettering for the Virgin MP OV has been covered by the halo. She is Mary of Seven Sorrows and the swords are also covered by the metal. Stunning.

The Jesus icon is one of our own. We wrote directly on the pewter.

# CUTTING EMBELISHMENTS TO FIT

One more example about the process. When you have finished your painting and want to apply an embossed metal embellishment begin with a paper design. Place a sheet of tracing paper over the area you want to have your design. Gently outline the head and halo circumference. This will give you the exact parameters to work in. Then work out your pattern or design while off the painted surface.

When you have a finished design and ready to trace it onto the metal REMEM-BER TO TURN YOUR PAPER DESIGN OVER. Trace the design onto the metal and make a note which side is up and which side is down. Yes I have said this before. Begin by pushing the metal out to the side that has no etch marks. It is a challenge to get the mind to think in reverse.

After you have pushed out the design and flattened all the areas you are ready to cut. Cut the design away from the metal with the flat background side down on the glass. Use the filler and let it dry over night. Place glue on the back and place it carefully on the work. Try not to let the glue seep onto your painting.

# DESIGNING BY LOOKING
# AT ANCIENT EXAMPLES

Cutting out hollow spaces is not too advanced, carefully cutting out the spaces takes most of the time and care not to destroy your work. You will master cutting curves, corners, and short strokes through practice. Try several tools to see whcih one fits your style. Getting to know which tool does what is part of the mastery of tooling metal. One exciting thing to remember when designing is where you will cut and what will remain behind. Gold, silver, mirror, or paint are all options to leave revealed spaces in a design. Be inspired by the work of ancient artists that have used this medium for church decorations around the world.   The example on the left is one of ours. I have showed you the original that inspired the contemporary. Book covers, candle sticks, icons, and many embellishments of beauty all take on certain design forms and styles.

# COLLECTION
## *Two Ancient Iconography Techniques by Two Talented Artists:*

Repousse is a French word meaning, "to push". The silver embellishments on the contemporary icons are 100% hand tooled pewter. Valentin Gomez, my husband and artistic partner, dedicates himself to all the metal embossing on my icons. He is a master craftsman meticulously pushing the metal into relief forms and shapes enhancing the sacred painted images. I work out all the paper designs on vellum. The design is fit to an already finished icon, waxed or oiled. All work is archival using the finest materials to bring about the richest quality icon. Each of our repousse designs and icons is individually tooled, created with fine earth pigments, organic gesso, and 23kt gold on a hardwood board.

This last section of the book includes a stunning collection of our finished work produced through the use of the templates offered above. Although the templates will not be an exact fit for any icon without some adjustments, I am sure you will find it useful to compare a line drawing to a finished icon for size. You can also trace a pattern directly from the finished work. I have on occasion found examples of estano in books and used the vellum paper to trace the pattern idea to use later. I always recommend researching icons found in early collections from museums and monasteries.

Iconographers throughout history have used ingenious designs and formats that are inspiring places to begin your search for images and motifs. I continually collect designs from many places for inspiration and reference.

Above Mary Offering the Chirst Child   12" x 13"
Right The Annuciation  15" x 20"

ANNUNCIATION

Incredulity of Thomas  12" x 17"

On Pages 22 and 23 you will find designs for a strip or band of embellishment. A whole series looks consistent and professional by using just a little bit of Estano /Repouse to enhance your work.

Templates and Beginner Techniques

Valentin Gomez

Mary of Tenderness  15" x  18"

Mary Jane Miller

43

Christ Enthroned  14 " x  20"

Templates and Beginner Techniques

Christ Pantochrator  15" x 17"

Mary of Tenderness  12" x 12"

Templates and Beginner Techniques

Mary of the Sign  15" x 20"

Blue Mary of Tenderness  16" x  20"

Templates and Beginner Techniques

Saint George   14" x  16"

Man of Sorrows  11" x  14"

Templates and Beginner Techniques

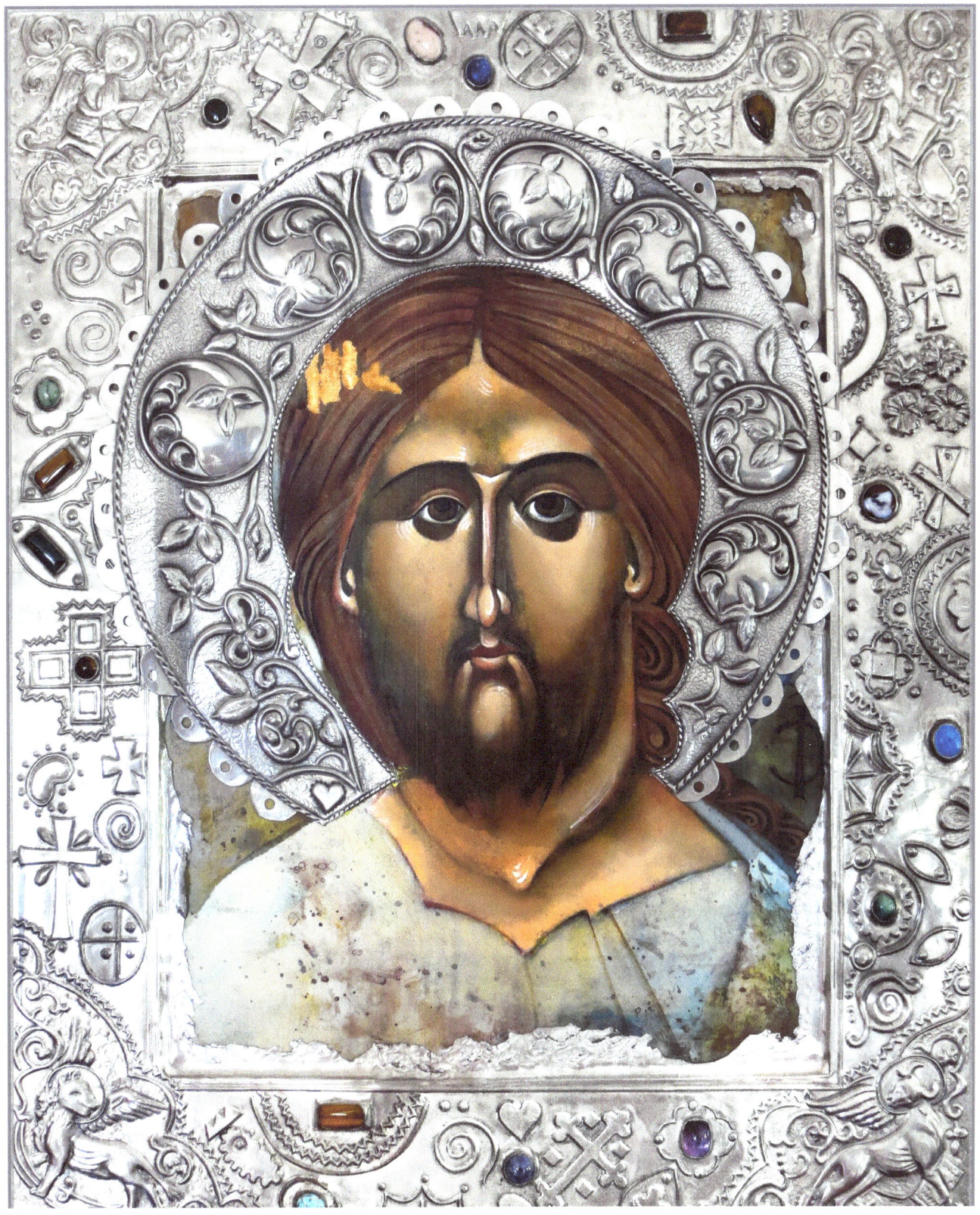

Child Jesus  14" x  16"

# ABOUT THE AUTHOR

Mary Jane Miller was born in New York. in 1954. She and her husband, Valentin Gomez, have been full time artists for 40 years, living in Mexico. Mary Jane teaches the Art of Icon Writing as a prayer form as well as the daily dedication to the work in her studio and to peace on earth.
Websites:
millericons.com
sacrediconretreat.com
sanmiguelicons.com

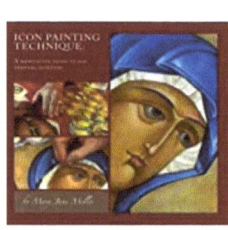 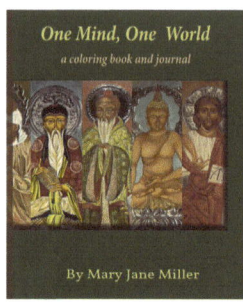 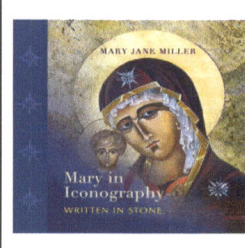 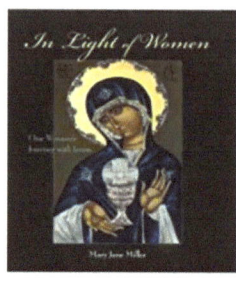 

### Published Books

**Mary in Iconography,** This collection of Mary icons captures the mysteries of the Madonna, drawing attention to the relationship between Mary and Christ, and the viewer. A wide range of imagination and potential is explored in this tiny book.

**Icon Painting Technique:** A Meditation and Guide to Egg Tempera, explains the subtle relationship between the process of icon painting and how it reflects and enriches one's spiritual life.

**Ancient Image, Sacred Lines,** contains icon templates for painting and drawing. Each template is drawn out with space beside to document insights and thoughts.

**One Mind, One World,** is a coloring book with line drawings from The Dialogue—an art installation with images of great religious leaders and philosophers, which promotes peace on earth and the idea we are all one.

**In Light of Women** her collection of women's image in iconography created as an exploration of their voices and portrayal in the church. Vibrant text describing each images history, religiouscontext and her own reflections about the world we live in today.

## RESOURCES

MATERIALS
Supplies and Accessories  https://www.texasart.com/category/79/metal-tooling.html

Copper & Metal Tooling https://www.amazon.com/Copper-Metal-Tooling-Lynn-Paulin/dp/B001F58A2O

Ten Second Studios:  Basic Tool Set
Mister Art:  They carry several tools.  See Link here:  Various Embossing Tools
Merc Art USA  www.mercartusa.com/icat/icat.htm
Molds   https://www.cooltools.us/

Embossing Metal Foil      http://www.dickblick.com/products/pure-metal-tooling-foil/
Designs        https://www.tes.com/lessons/g55B6Exqjr8BzQ/metal-tooling-book-covers
Making Embossing Paste      https://www.youtube.com/watch?v=nZlUJOBeF1U
Making Your Own Texture Paste     https://www.youtube.com/watch?v=r-QbvXhaFEQ

READ ABOUT

Hobby https://myhusbandhastoomanyhobbies.com/metal-embossing-basics-metal-tools/#more

YOU TUBE

How to book on Metal tooling
https://www.google.com/search?client=firefox-b-d&q=how+to+books+on+metal+tooling%2C+repouose
+or+esatno#kpvalbx=_Lg3-XrLhFIy5tAbH74XoBQ22

How to emboss metal
https://www.google.com/search?client=firefox-b-d&q=how+to+emboss+metal#kpvalbx=_8g7-XsH4I-
72E9PwPzc-MgAU29

Pewter It with Sandy Griffiths
  https://www.youtube.com/watch?v=lb14_XxIBN8

Metal Embossing with Pewter
https://www.youtube.com/watch?v=1sqnxrj9h7c

Chasing and Repousse series #6
https://www.youtube.com/watch?v=Abk2l9pClQw

Very good one in Spanish
https://www.youtube.com/watch?v=doMg86joVSs

Using an Aluminum Can
  https://www.youtube.com/watch?v=iKKd2xHiMS

*Peace Be Still*

www.ingramcontent.com/pod-product-compliance
Lightning Source LLC
Chambersburg PA
CBHW041553120626

46551CB00002B/197